Inside a Coral Reef

Carole Telford and

Rod Theodorou

Heinemann Interactive Library
Des Plaines, Illinois

Published by Heinemann Interactive Library,
an imprint of Reed Educational & Professional Publishing Ltd,
1350 East Touhy Avenue, Suite 240 West, Des Plaines, IL 60018

Printed and bound in China

Illustrated by Stephen Lings and Jane Pickering at Linden Artists

Designed by Aricot Vert Design Ltd

02 01 00 99 98

10 9 8 7 6 5 4 3 2 1

Library of Congress Cataloging-in-Publication Data

Theodorou, Rod
    Inside a coral reef / Rod Theodorou and Carole Telford.
      p.   cm. -- (Amazing journeys)
    Includes bibliographical references and index.
    Summary: Describes the physical characteristics and ecosystem of a coral reef and how such a habitat may be conserved.
    ISBN 1-57572-154-6
    1. Coral reef ecology--Australia--Great Barrier Reef (Qld.)--Juvenile literature.   2. Coral reef animals--Australia--Great Barrier Reef (Qld.)--Juvenile literature.   3. Coral reefs and islands--Australia--Great Barrier Reef (Qld.)--Juvenile literature.
[1. Coral reefs and islands. 2. Coral reef ecology 3. Ecology]
I. Telford, Carole, 1961- . II. Title. III. Series: Theodorou, Rod. Amazing journeys.
QH197.T45 1997
577.7'89--dc21

97-16750
CIP
AC

Acknowledgments

The author and publishers are grateful to the following for permission to reproduce copyright photographs:

Ardea (D. Parer and E. Parer-Cook) pp. 6, 17 (top), 26, (Mike Osmond) p. 25 (top), (Ron and Valerie Taylor) pp. 13 (bottom), 14, 19 (bottom), 21 (bottom), 24, (Valerie Taylor) p. 25 (bottom), (A.D. Trounson and M.C. Clampett) p. 15 (bottom), (A. Warren) p. 11 (top); FLPA (C. Carvalho) p. 23 (bottom), (D. Fleetham/Silvestris) p. 27, (T. and P. Gardner) p. 10; NHPA (Cyril Webster) p. 15 (top), (Bill Wood) p. 20; OSF (Fred Bavendam) pp. 19 (top), 21 (top), 23 (top), (David B. Fleetham) p. 17 (bottom), (Babs and Bert Wells) p. 11 (bottom), (Norbert Wu) p. 13 (top).

Cover photograph: Oxford Scientific Films

Our thanks to Rob Alcraft for his comments in the preparation of this book.

Every effort has been made to contact copyright holders of any material reproduced in this book. Any omissions will be rectified in subsequent printings if notice is given to the publisher.

Some words are shown in bold letters, **like this**. You can find out what these words mean by looking in the Glossary.

Contents

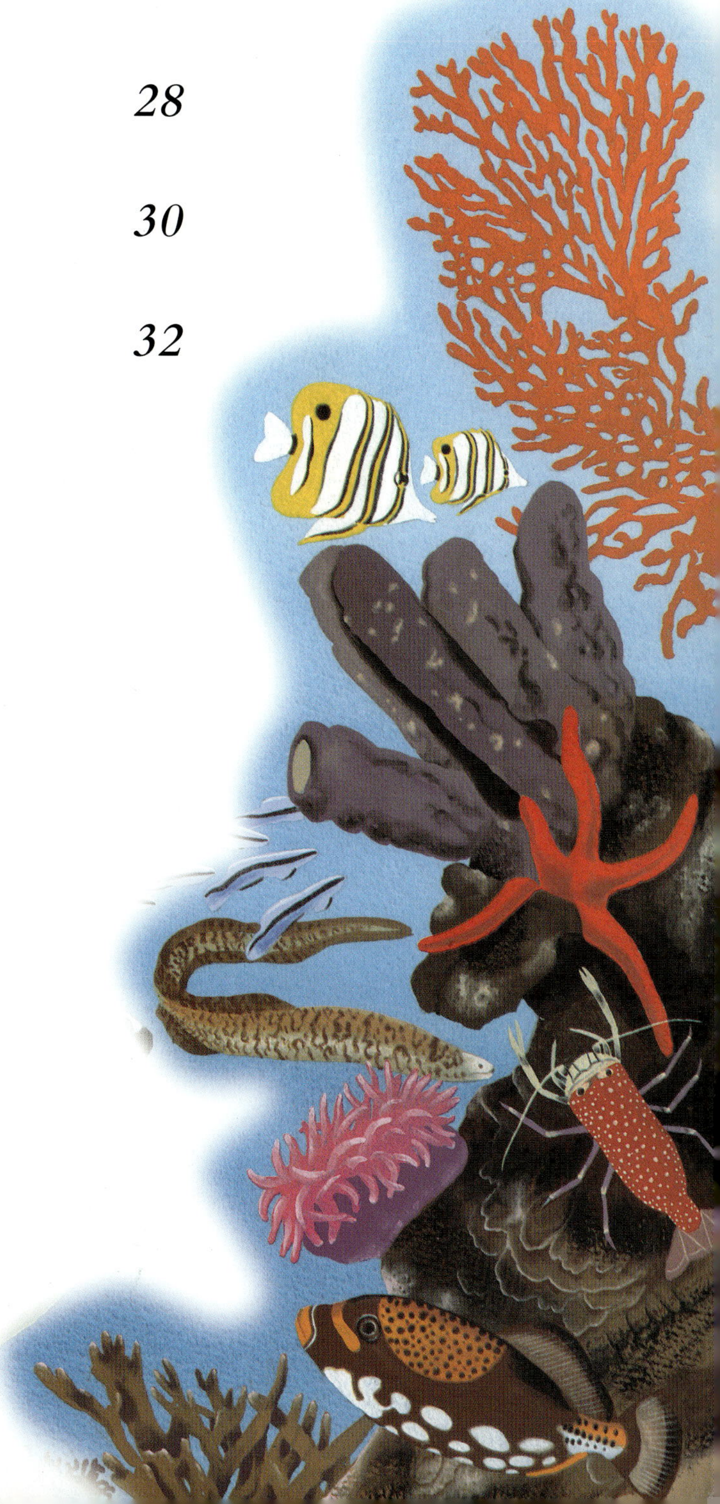

Introduction

You are about to go on an amazing journey. You are going to visit one of the greatest natural wonders of the world: the Great Barrier Reef. This is the largest of all coral reefs, stretching for more than 1,200 miles around the north-east coast of Australia. It is made by tiny little animals called corals.

You will begin your journey on the hot, dry sands of a coral island. You will then enter the warm, shallow waters of the reef and swim into a wonderful underwater garden of colors. On your way, you will see some of the 5,000 **species** of animals and plants that make their home in this amazing world.

This photo was taken from an airplane. It shows one of the many reefs that make up the Great Barrier Reef.

6

Reefs are made by tiny sea creatures called coral polyps. Polyps are tiny, soft-bodied animals, smaller than a match head. Each polyp builds a small, rocky **skeleton** around itself. When it dies, the skeleton is left behind. Other polyps build their skeletons on top of it. Over thousands of years, millions of these skeletons form huge, rocky reefs. Scientists think the Great Barrier Reef began forming more than 30 million years ago.

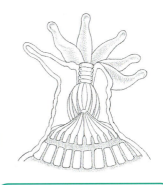

Coral polyp

Many fish and other sea creatures eat the polyps and find places to hide among the coral. More animals live among coral reefs than anywhere else in the oceans.

Coral reefs grow in warm seas all over the world.

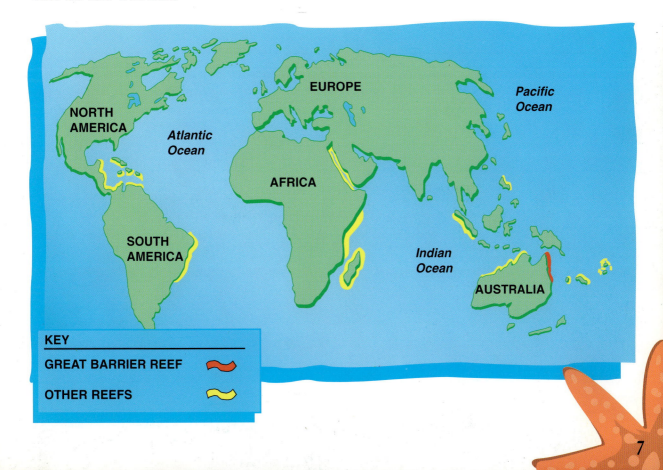

EUROPE

Pacific Ocean

NORTH AMERICA

Atlantic Ocean

AFRICA

SOUTH AMERICA

Indian Ocean

AUSTRALIA

KEY

GREAT BARRIER REEF

OTHER REEFS

Journey Map

Coral Island

Page 10

Beach

Page 12

Reef Flat

Here is a map of our journey. We start on a coral island, which has been made by **fragments** of broken coral being pushed by waves onto a high part of the reef. An island like this takes thousands of years to form. In front of the island is a shallow stretch of water called the **reef flat**, ending at the **reef crest**. Beyond that we will swim down the outer slopes of the reef where most of the corals and other sea creatures live.

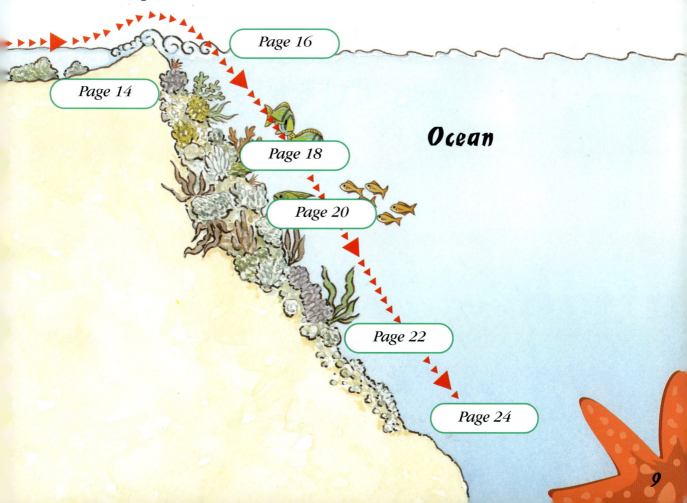

Reef Crest

Ocean

Page 16

Page 14

Page 18

Page 20

Page 22

Page 24

On a Coral Island

We are standing on the hot, white sand of a coral island. The fierce summer sun beats down on our necks. It is always hot here, even in the middle of winter. If we scoop up a handful of sand and look at it closely, we see it is made of tiny **fragments** of coral and shell.

Birds hurry out of our way. Many are looking for the worms that live in the sand. Some search the beach for washed-up jellyfish and other dead creatures. Behind us, past the sand dunes, bushes, and trees, are thousands of nesting birds, filling the air with their noisy squawks.

This is Heron Island.
There are thousands of coral islands, called cays, in the Great Barrier Reef.

White-breasted sea eagle

This large bird snatches fish from the surface of the sea and steals chicks from other birds' nests. Because of people visiting coral islands and disturbing these birds, they are now quite **rare**.

White-capped noddy

This beautiful bird makes ugly, untidy nests in trees, but its droppings make the soil richer. It also carries seeds of other trees to the island.

Green turtles ⟶

Once a year, female green turtles come onto the beach to dig holes and lay their eggs. Two or three months later, the baby turtles hatch and crawl toward the sea. Many are eaten by **predators**.

The Reef Flat

Time for a swim! We wade into the water and swim out into the **reef flat**. The water here is only about 3 feet deep and very warm. It is a difficult place for coral to live. At **low tide**, there is a chance that the coral will be left in the open air and dry out. This would kill most types of coral, which need to stay under water to survive.

However, some corals do manage to live and grow here. They form little coral islands on the sandy sea bed. Many creatures live in the warm, shallow water among them. We must be careful not to step on stingrays, which hide in the sand. They have sharp, poisonous **barbs** on their tails.

jelly fish

angel fish

parrot fish

spiny lobster

brittle star

wrasse

sea urchin

star fish

crab

cowrie

sponges

Mantis shrimp

This beautifully colored shrimp is a fierce hunter and fighter. It is only about 6 inches long, but is can shoot its **pincers** forward so fast they can smash open a crab's shell.

Sea cucumber →

These strange animals use rows of little feet to crawl over the coral. They have **tentacles** at one end of their bodies, that they use to catch tiny, floating sea creatures which they eat.

Sea snails

Many sea snails live on the reef flat. The hard shells protect the soft creatures inside from being eaten. They move slowly over the coral, feeding off the **algae** growing there.

The Reef Crest

As we reach the edge of the **reef flat**, we can see the white foam of waves, breaking against the **reef crest**. This is where the top of the reef meets the open sea. As waves crash against the reef crest, they break off the coral and wash it into the reef flat. There is a lot of broken coral lying around here. Storms will break off even more.

At first we cannot see any signs of life. Can anything live in this wild place? Then we spot some giant limpets clinging to the rocks. Even the biggest waves cannot knock them off. Each has a "foot", which sucks it onto the rocks. At **low tide**, they crawl over the rock eating **algae**.

More than 3 inches across, these giant limpets can cling on to the rocks, despite the crashing waves at high tide.

Hermit crab →

This small crab lives inside empty shells. It comes out to feed on dead animals thrown onto the rubble at the reef crest. When it grows too big for its shell, it simply finds a new, larger shell to crawl into.

Reef heron

At low tide, the reef heron may wade along the rocky reef crest looking for prey in the water. It uses its long, sharp beak to stab fish or shrimp.

Stonefish →

Piles of rock and broken coral make a good hiding place for the stonefish. It waits among the rocks for smaller fish to come near enough for it to gobble them up. Stepping on a stonefish can be very painful. It has poisonous spines on its back to protect it from **predators**.

Among the Coral

We are swimming downward along a gentle slope, away from the crest. The water is calm and warm. Many different types of coral can grow here, safe from the crashing waves above. There are two groups of coral: hard and soft. We can see hard corals such as brain coral. These are the corals that leave the rocky **skeletons** behind and that build the reef. Soft corals do not make these hard, rocky shells. They grow upward in a mass of delicate branches that reach out into the water. They are also the most colorful of all the corals.

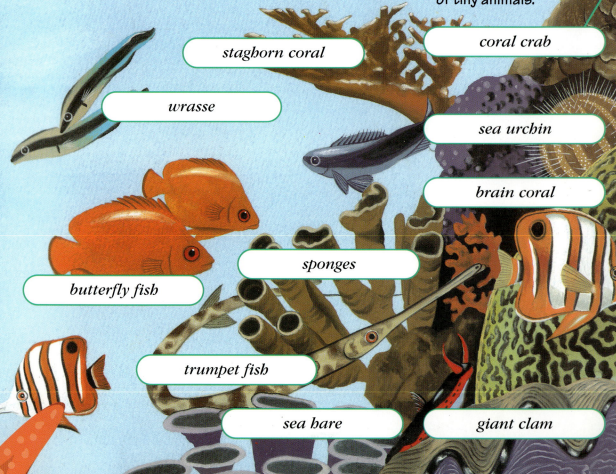

sea horses

There are more than 400 species of coral on the reef. It is hard to believe that each one is a community of millions of tiny animals.

coral crab

staghorn coral

wrasse

sea urchin

brain coral

sponges

butterfly fish

trumpet fish

sea hare

giant clam

Giant clam

The giant clam is a huge animal that can grow up to $4\frac{1}{2}$ feet wide! It lives on the reef, sucking water in to **filter** out **zooplankton**, which it eats. This clam is sending out a cloud of eggs.

Gorgonian coral

This beautiful soft coral grows in a great fan, which sways in the current. Like all corals, it eats zooplankton. Each coral polyp catches the zooplankton with its tiny **tentacles**.

Cleaner wrasse

This fish gets its food in an unusual way. Other fish let the wrasse nibble around their mouths and **gills**. The wrasse picks off **parasites** and cleans the fish, helping it to stay healthy. In return, the wrasse gets a meal!

Going Deeper

We continue to swim down among the corals. Sunlight filters down through the water, so we can still see clearly. **Anemones** wave their beautiful but stinging **tentacles** in the current. Bright flashes of color dart away as we swim. These are **shoals** of fish that live on the reef. Their narrow shape helps them slip easily between the coral to escape being eaten. Many are brightly colored with stripes and spots. This makes them harder to see when they swim among the colorful coral. We see the long, black shape of a moray eel as it twists back into a hole.

branching coral

reef shark

star fish

sponges

wrasse

clown fish

moray eel

anemones

coral shrimp

trigger fish

Clown fish →

Anemones catch fish with their stinging tentacles. The clown fish covers itself with a special slime that protects it from the stings. It lives among the tentacles, eating the leftovers from the anemone's meals.

Trumpet fish

This strange fish hides behind big plant-eating fish. When smaller fish come close, it suddenly shoots forward and eats them. Then it hides among branching coral with its tail up in the water so it is **camouflaged** from **predators**.

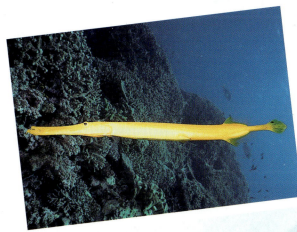

Moray eel →

This large hunter can squeeze and twist through holes and small spaces to chase out smaller, sleepy fish.

The Reef at Night

We have returned to the reef at night. The water is colder. There is nothing but darkness all around us. It is a strange feeling. The reef looks very different, lit by the beams of our underwater flashlights. Many of the fish we saw during the day are sleeping. They are hidden in the holes and cracks between the rocks.

Some fish come out only at night. The light from our flashlight catches a soldier fish in its beam. It quickly swims away. It will hide among the coral until it feels safe to come out and feed on **plankton**. The corals are even more colorful at night. Many of the coral polyps open out to feed in the darkness. There is less risk of a hungry fish biting off their **tentacles**.

At night our flashlights light up a mass of colorful feeding coral polyps.

Crown-of-thorns

This large starfish feeds at night on the coral polyps. It can destroy large areas of reef. Its arms are covered with poisonous, sharp spines that protect it from being eaten.

Soldier fish

The soldier fish is a small fish with large eyes that help it to see at night. It hides in caves during the day, and feeds on **plankton** at night when it is safer.

Lion fish

This beautiful lion fish is covered with poisonous spines. It comes out at night and swims slowly through the reef looking for sleeping fish to attack.

Down the Slope

It is daytime again, and we are diving deeper down the sloping reef front. It is harder for the sun's light to reach down here. We can see different **species** of coral that can live in this gloomy light. As we swim deeper and deeper, we see more and more sponges. At last there are no corals growing. It is simply too dark at this depth for them to grow. The current is strong here, and the water is colder. Turning away from the coral we look out into the open sea. There are dark shadows moving out there.

green turtle

sharks

potato cod

butterfly fish

wrasse

biscuit starfish

sponges

moray eel

octopus

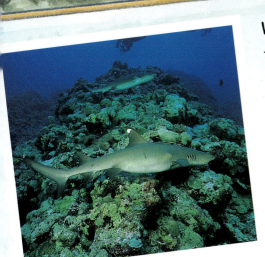

White-tip sharks

These grayish-brown sharks swim around the gloomy reef edge, then dart in among the fish to attack. They look frightening, but, like most sharks, white-tips never attack people.

Sponges

Sponges look like plants but are actually animals. They suck water in and out of holes to **filter zooplankton**. Many types of sponges live on reefs, including these large barrow sponges.

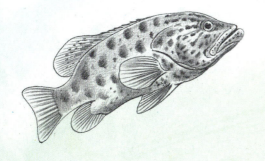

Potato cod

These huge fish (sometimes called groupers) can grow up to 6 feet long. All potato cod are born females. They change into males when they grow to full size.

The Drop-off

We have reached the end of the reef, which is like a cliff edge. Below us is nothing but blackness. A few sponges grow on the cliff sides, but there is no living coral. Around us is the dark, cold world of the open ocean. We see a strange, bat-like shadow gliding above us. It is a huge manta ray, attracted by the bubbles from our breathing apparatus. Long, silver barracuda pass slowly by, hunting for fish. It is time to return to the surface.

Manta rays suck in water through their huge mouths to filter out plankton.

24

Sea snake

These poisonous snakes have flattened tails to help them swim. They come to the surface to breathe air but can then swim deep into the ocean, holding their breath for as long as eight hours!

Humpback whale

Each year humpback whales make the long journey from the cold Antarctic to the warm waters of the Great Barrier Reef to breed. Adults grow up to 50 feet long and communicate with squeals and moans called whale songs.

Barracuda

These big, fierce fish grow up to 6 feet long and have teeth like spears. They usually hunt in packs. Sometimes, a single barracuda will follow a scuba-diver for some time, but they very rarely attack.

Conservation and the Future

The Great Barrier Reef, along with other coral reefs in the world, is in danger. Storms cause some damage, but most threats come from people. Pollution from farming, industry, and shipping can poison the coral polyps. Fishermen and divers kill fish and gather corals and shells to sell to tourists. The crown-of-thorns starfish is usually attacked and eaten by the giant triton shell, pufferfish, and triggerfish. But many of these **predators** have been killed by humans, allowing the starfish to grow in numbers. Now thousands of these starfish are destroying huge stretches of reef.

A storm has devastated this reef. It will take many years to grow again.

26

Protecting the Reef

As we learn more about coral reefs, we realize that most kinds of sea animals feed on other animals. By robbing the reef of coral, shells, or fish, we can do terrible damage. To protect the reef, the Great Barrier Reef Marine Park Authority now has rules about how the reef is used. They stop people from harming the reef and study the effects of pollution on the coral polyps. By learning more about the fascinating world of the coral reef, we can understand how to protect these amazing places for many years to come.

The Great Barrier Reef Marine Park is a huge area of reef that is protected for the future.

Glossary

algae	These are very small plants that live in water.
anemone	This is a soft, jelly-like animal.
barbs	These are sharp hooks.
camouflaged	This means to be colored or shaped in a way that makes an animal hard to see.
dune	This is a hill of sand piled up by the wind.
filter	This means to sieve out.
fragments	These are tiny broken pieces.
gills	These are parts of a fish that let it get oxygen from water.
low tide	This is the point when the sea is furthest from the beach.
parasites	These are animals or plants that live in or on other plants and animals.
pincer	This is a gripping claw.
plankton	These are tiny plants and animals that live drifting in ocean currents.
predator	This is an animal that hunts and kills other animals for food.
rare	This means seldom seen or not very many are left.
reef crest	This is the rocky edge of the reef flat, where the reef meets the sea.
reef flat	This is the shallow part of a reef.

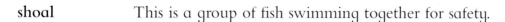

shoal	This is a group of fish swimming together for safety.
skeleton	This is a hard frame for a soft body.
species	This is a group of living things that are very similar.
tentacle	This is the soft part of coral, which bends and feels for food.
zooplankton	These are tiny creatures that are eaten by coral polyps.

More Books to Read

Barrett, Norman S. *Coral Reef.* New York: Watts. 1991.

Cooper, Jason. *Coral Reefs.* Rourke Corp. 1992.

The Earthworks Group. *50 Simple Things Kids Can do to Save the Earth.* New York: Jay Street/Little Brown, 1992.

Ferrier, Lucy. *Diving the Great Barrier Reef.* Mahwah, N.J.: Troll Communications, 1976.

Gouck, Maura M. *The Great Barrier Reef.* Plymouth, Minn: Child's World. 1993.

Holing, Dwight. *Coral Reefs.* Morristown, N.J.: Silver Burdett Press, 1994.

McGovern, Ann. *Down Under, Down Under: Diving Adventures on the Great Barrier Reef.* New York: Simon & Schuster, 1989.

Wood, Jenny. *Coral Reefs.* Milwaukee: Gareth Stevens Inc., 1991.

Other Resources

Audio Recordings

Chapin, Tom. *Mother Earth.* A & M Records.

Raffi. Evergreen, *Everblue.* Troubadour Records.

Rogers, Sally. *Piggyback Planet: Songs for a Whole Earth.* Round River Records.

Video Recordings

Understanding Ecology Series: *What is a Food Chain?* Coronet © 1992. VHS, 11 minutes. (Also available on videodisk.)

Understanding Ecology Series: *What is a Habitat?* Coronet © 1991. VHS, 13 minutes. (Also available on videodisk.)

Understanding Ecology Series: *What is an Ecosystem?* Coronet © 1992. VHS, 11 minutes. (Also available on videodisk.)

Organizations

The Cousteau Society
70 Greenbrier Circle, Suite 402
Chesapeake, VA 23320
Tel (757) 523-9335

Great Barrier Reef Marine Park Authority
1-37 Flinders Street East
P.O. Box 1379
Townsville, Queensland 4810, Australia

Greenpeace
1436 U Street NW
Washington, D.C. 20009
Tel. (202) 462-1177

National Wildlife Federation
8925 Leesburg Pike
Vienna, VA 22184
Tel (703) 790-4100

Nature Conservancy
International Headquarters
1815 North Lynn Street
Arlington, Virginia 22209
Tel (703) 841-5300

River Watch Network
153 State Street
Montpelier, VT 05602
Tel (802) 223-3840

Sierra Club
85 Second Street, Second Floor
San Francisco, CA 94105-3441
Tel 415-977-5500

Index